Inner Feelings

Robin M. Laycock-Morris

Bloomington, IN  Milton Keynes, UK

AuthorHouse™
1663 Liberty Drive, Suite 200
Bloomington, IN 47403
www.authorhouse.com
Phone: 1-800-839-8640

© *2007 Robin M. Laycock-Morris. All rights reserved.*

No part of this book may be reproduced, stored in a retrieval system, or transmitted by any means without the written permission of the author.

First published by AuthorHouse 8/8/2007

ISBN: 978-1-4343-0093-5 (sc)

Printed in the United States of America
Bloomington, Indiana

This book is printed on acid-free paper.

This book is dedicated to

My Beloved Husband Stephen A. Morris

Eber and Emma Collins
My grandparents who took me in an raised me
Who in my Heart will always be my Parents.

Ralph and Laura Laycock
My biological father and my step mother
Both whom I Love very much.

Joanne M. Collins
My biological mother who I Love very Dearly.

To my children who I Love with all my
Heart and Soul Allen, Tami and Matthew
Also Linna and Nathanial
Two of our Grandchildren Steve and I adopted

Also To all my Grandchildren, Family and Friends

List of Poems

Inner Pride	3
Special Memories	5
Prayers Of Love	6
Your Sanity	7
Through Child's Eyes	8
Sweet Parents	9
My Dad's Birthday	9
Believe	10
Till Time Stands Still	11
Angry Words	12
Mixed Feelings	13
Free Spirit	15
Turn To Stone	16
Believe In Yourself	17
Glimmer Of Light	19
Begin To Pray	21
Arms Length	22
Trying To Cope	23
Nature And People	24
Better At Last	25
All God's Creatures	27
Mended Souls	28
Back Together	29
Your Tension	31
Dangerous Opposition	32
The Great Indian Chief	35
My Guiding Star	36
Impatiently Waiting	37
Loneliness	38
Desperate Decision	39

Feelings Of Suffering	40
Your One True Escape	41
Life Stays The Same	42
As Long As Hate Flows	43
Small Ray Of Hope	44
Differences	45
With Heavy Hearts	46
First Love	47
A Special Man	48
Day-By-Day	49
Sacred Indian Burial Grounds	50
Watch Over Me	53
Mother Earth And The Indian's	54
Past, Present and Future	55
In The Indian's Shoes	57
To My Daughter	58
To My Son	59
Always Know	60
Let's Try Peace	61
Peaceful Feelings	63
Invisible	64
All My Might	65
Past Love	66
Missing You	67
Please Forgive Me	69
I Will Be Gone	70
My Soul Cry's	71
Humiliation And Hope	72
Search For My Heritage	73
Love Is A Feeling	74
The Hurt Inside	75
My Haunting Dreams	76

Preface

    The poetry in this book depicts the emotional times in my life. When I felt like I was at the bottom of the barrel, and could not get out. It was during those times that I started writing down my thoughts. They just came out on paper in poetry form. I wrote them with positive endings, because it helped me get through each new day. Writing poetry was therapeutic for me even though I did not realize it until later on in my life.

    I have put these poems in book form so others will know that like me they can hang in there, and find that there is a positive ending waiting for them. I tell everyone that GOD gave me this wonderful gift so I might help others that feel as lost and lonely as I did.

    To help People know that life is what you make it, so make life a blessing for yourself and those you love. It may be family, friends or others who came into your life. My prayer is that as you read the poetry in this book you enjoy them, and listen to what is being expressed within them.

Inner Pride

When someone says something
that makes you feel low,
do what you want
even if they say no.

What people say
will change the way,
you think of yourself
day-by-day,

You will love yourself or hate yourself
according to what they say,
you will be glad or you will be sad
on this and everyday.

The influence on you will be amazing
no matter what you do,
you will do good or you will do bad
but to yourself be true.

Take it in stride
and do not hide for I will tell you true,
if you listen to what they say
you will regret it each and everyday.

So do me a favor
do not listen to neighbors or friends,
when they criticize
just pay attention to me and I will set you free
To Save Your "Inner Pride"

The poem "Special Memories" was published in the International Library Of Poetry, the name of this book is "Days Of Future Past". Published in 1990. This poem was written for my Aunt Janice who is more like a sister to me.

Special Memories

Memories are as good as gold,
they are special things that's what I am told.
To remember is a wondrous thing,
to bring them back by imagining.

That what was then is now again,
as long as I am remembering.
A time when everything was fine,
when things in life was so sublime.

When memories where pleasant ones,
at a time when things where truly fun.
When we were still so very young,
and ambition never hurt us none.

When exploring was an exciting thing,
I love to do until days end.
I think of people way back then,
that I may never see again.

The remembrance yet seem so real,
that I can always keep them near.
Remembering the days gone bye,
can bring a tear to my eye.

But Please remember just one thing,
the future that with time shall bring.

Prayers Of Love

Lonely days and trying ways,
of people that are around.
When fighting stays with angry ways,
that always brings you down.

It seems that pain is here to stay,
with loving ways gone a stray.
Where happiness and good cheer,
never seems to be real near.

I search for love with an empty heart,
hoping for a brand new start.
Wishing to find someone in time,
that will bring true love back to mind.

To help me find a hopeful sign,
that happy times may soon be mine.
I wish the lies would surely die,
before my heart breaks inside.

The pain I have carried for many years,
is surfacing now with plenty of fears.
Hoping for everything good out of life,
but finding things are not so nice.

I will just keep on dreaming
for things to get better,
with Prayers of Love
that really do matter.

Your Sanity

Everyday in different ways,
people can tear you apart.
With angry words that you have heard,
everyday from the start.

With all the pain and happiness,
with all the love and fear.
With all the hate and hopefulness,
that you tend to hold so near.

The feelings you have bottled up,
are trying to break free.
As you hang on tight with all your might,
to keep your sanity.

Your heart says no just let them go,
to give love one more try.
Yet it seems that people you really care for,
always pass you bye.

With the love inside that you try to hide,
from people that get to near.
To keep yourself from getting hurt,
with a heart that's full of fear.

Just take my word with what you have heard,
life is not so bad.
For love is near to take your fear,
and fill you up with pride.

Through Child's Eyes

Through child's eyes I see myself
as I stand in front of my mirror,
an older face took the place
of the one from my past years.

Looking into a face unknown
of someone full of fear,
as I stare into those eyes
I see a trace of early tears.

The sadness there in that maddening stare
was more then I could take,
then I realize that in those eyes
was love an that's no fake.

Now the love I have held inside
is trying to escape,
to show me that there is a special person
behind that older face.

Someone who is very kind
with really gentle ways,
so through child's eyes I recognized
myself in one last gaze.

Sweet Parents

On this beautiful day in a special way
my love for you shines through,
with my heart all a glow from the love that you show
in everything you do.

You make me glad when I am sad
and smile when I am blue,
you show your love in so many ways
it's always just like new.

So please never change always say the same
Sweet Parents I love you true.

My Dad's Birthday

Happy birthday from me to you,
best wish's are sent with lots of joy too.
With a heart filled with love for you on this day,
always remember my loves here to stay.

Believe

Through all the love and hate we have seen
with all the things in between.
by dwelling on the past you might be mistaken
but never will you be forsaken.

For love runs deeper then hate ever could,
and in my eyes this is good.
for hate only conquers the weak and the small
while love given out can rescue us all.

So believe in emotions that make you feel proud
they are the ones that should be spoken out loud.
To show all the others who have lost their way
that the thing to do is begin to pray.

For prayer is the answer that everyone seeks
it is there for both the strong and the meek.
To bring out the love and destroy the hate
so one day we will meet at the "Pearly Gates".

Till Time Stands Still

All Though we are miles apart
you are still very near to my heart,
all of the things we have done together
we will remember now and forever.

When we were young and so carefree
we enjoyed life to its potential,
so here we are now we have gone separate ways
but still our bond is substantial.

With feelings like these we could never go wrong
they will build our faith to make us strong,
to face what is coming in both future and present
we will try our hardest to make them both pleasant.

We will do what we can or do what we will,
to make our lives better till time stands still.

Angry Words

As the words flowed out like water from a spout
as they cut deep with in my soul,
I am bleeding inside where it surely can hide
as the pain there takes control.

With a heavy heart when words do start
praying they will go away,
knowing they are said with anger filled heads
from those who should make me feel love instead.

As love that I have kept flows out with each step
as I wear my heart on my sleeve,
praying for a better day
when things might go my way.

As I try to cope with lots of hope
for things to get a lot better,
hoping one day I will be able to say
all the hurt I am feeling has gone away.

Until that day the hurt will stay,
till the angry words go away.

Mixed Feelings

I do not know who I am anymore
sometimes I feel like a child,
hiding underneath my blankets
afraid when things get to wild.

Other times I feel so old
I would like to set in a rocker,
staying there for the rest of my life
without having a proctor.

I also feel like a middle aged woman
having mixed feelings about myself,
feeling sexy at one time then dirty another
wishing for answers that can come from no other.

My remembrance of past relationships
makes me feel this way,
I just hope these feelings I have about men
with fade away someday.

I feel the need to be held by someone
to know that they are near,
but still I hold back from feelings like that
because of all my fears.

The personality of my child inside
is trying to escape,
but the grown up in me will not set her free
to have fun and face her fate.

The poem "Free Spirit" was published in
The International Library Of Poetry, the name
of the book is "Of Diamonds And Rust",
Published in 1989.

Free Spirit

What is a free spirit I ask myself
time and time again,
nature shows me in many ways
as I watch until days end.

It is an eagle in flight
with in our sight,
with its head held high
souring across clear blue skies.

It is the buffalo on the endless plains
as they flourished till the white man came,
it is the mustangs as they run care free
as their mains and tails blow in the breeze.

It is the trees that grow straight and strong
when the winds do blow they will hum you a song,
it is the sun, the moon and all of heaven above
it is everything on earth that is truly loved.

It is people who care for one another,
making this world a little better.

Turn To Stone

As I sit alone crying inside
wishing the hurt would depart,
I keep telling myself everything will be fine
but I can not convince my heart.

For I have hurt so long in past years
that I hide my feelings behind swelled tears,
loneliness is second nature to me
and that seems like an eternity.

Sometimes my life seems out of control
as I say to myself should I crawl in a hole,
you can hide from the world for a very short time
but if you are gone to long that is a crime.

For life is to short and love is to sweet
to hide from a person you might want to meet,
the people who love you for who you are
they are the ones that are not very far.

So learn to let go of the hurt you have known,
or surely you heart will turn to stone.

Believe In Yourself

As you lie awake in your lonely room
filled with sadness and with gloom,
praying for someone to come along
who will be part of your life to make you strong.

With a gentle hand and a kind heart
who will not play games from the start,
to be honest as the day is long
with out lies that stab you like a prong.

As they pierce your soul with angry words
that drains your feelings with each one you have heard,
until it seems everything inside you is gone
never to return for eternity on.

You just keep on hoping until that day
when the one you are waiting for comes your way,
believe in yourself they will come in time
to make your life and world so sublime.

Glimmer Of Light

Darkness is a lonely place
like standing in an empty space,
it seems no matter which way you turn
the fear in you will begin to burn.

You hope for just a glimmer of light
to give you the strength so you can fight,
so the darkness will not take over your life
hoping the things you have learned will suffice.

Praying that love will come show you the way
so in the darkness you will not stay,
finding true love is a life long job
with past memories that still make you sob.

When you look forward in time
and stop looking back,
you can start being happy
when you have this knack.

So always remember your future is bright,
as long as your heart stays in the light.

Begin To Pray

All of the things we remember
all of the times we spent together,
all of the good times we had for sure
all of the bad times we had to endure.

Remember them fondly as the years pass bye
with all of the things that made us cry,
with a little hope and a lot of prayer
maybe we will find someone who is fair.

Someone to take our fears away
someone who will want to truly stay,
so we can find some happiness
and be treated with some tenderness.

Hoping for these things are very worth while
because these are the things that can make us smile,
until that day comes we have lost our way
this is the time we should begin to pray.

Arms Length

As you feel your life floating away
like a snow flake falling in elegant grace,
like a ray of sunshine that gleams through the trees
as you try to touch it your almost set free.

Like a bird that sores way up high
you feel you can almost reach the sky,
like the seas that are forever rolling
you feel pulled under as if you were falling.

Like the sun, the moon and the stars that shine
for a peaceful life you often pine,
like a spider that weaves its silken web
the never ending thoughts run through your head.

Like the buds of new leaves that begin to grow
you feel lots of hurt, anguish and woe,
with heavy heart you try to change your strife
and make for yourself a better life.

With everything that is in your strength
you reach out for your dreams,
but they are just out of arms length.

Trying To Cope

As my feelings keep on building
and my heart with hate is filling,
I am fighting my emotions
to keep up all my notions.

For life to be more promising
as I pray for each new day to end,
wondering what life will bring my way
praying that my troubles will not stay.

Trying to deal with problems of everyday
but it seems that things never go my way,
as the fighting that you hate so much
you fear of using as a crutch.

The hate inside has now died
and now the hurt has started to arise,
the pain sweeps over you with full force
it changes your life's entire course.

To leave you empty of all joy
people use these feelings as a ploy,
to tear you apart and destroy all hope
but do not give up on trying to cope.

Nature And People

As sure as the sun rises high in the sky
millions of people on earth will surely cry.
As the moon and the stars shimmer at night
there are people out there that are filled with fright.

As oceans run deep and miles wide
people sit alone because they are shy.
Like the trees that grow straight and strong
people will still go out and do wrong.

Like the clouds that float and drift with the wind
other people will go out and still sin.
Like the bird that sores and flies so free
some people are filled with anger and greed.

Like the dirt that covers mother earth
there are people out there with lots of worth.
Like the rainbow that shows itself after a storm
lots of people out there are being reborn.

Like the volcanos that are ready to erupt
there are people out there that live to corrupt.
As the mountain peeks reach for heaven above
thank GOD there are people still filled with love.

Better At Last

As the years past by we had time to cry
we also had time for saying good-bye.
So many times we fell in love
we were lifted high as a flying Dove.

When it did not last as we hoped it would
then we survive the best we could.
We would hide the pain from our hearts
trying to make some brand new starts.

No matter how hard we seem to try
we always ended up with lies.
They would hurt way down with in our souls
and make us stray from our goals.

With weary minds all full of pain
we felt as if we had nothing to gain.
The longer we live and the more we learn
about all of life's little corners and turns.

To cope with problems and deal with the past,
so our lives then can be made better at last.

All God's Creatures

With open eyes you realize how unfair life can be
as you watch, wait and hesitate praying to be free.
Hoping for better times yet to come
looking at all on this planet as one.

The wrongs done towards all of God's creatures
these are the things not taught by teachers.
Life is precious to behold
these are the things that should be told.

To watch two squirrels romp and play
jumping from tree branch, to tree branch all day.
Watching a deer as it bounds through a field
trying to keep from being revealed.

To the woods he will race as fast as he can
to hide himself away from man.
Listening on a warm summers night
hearing the frogs singing in the pale moon light.

Watching the stars twinkling in time
to let the world know everything is sublime.
Even the snake that slithers over this earth
yes, even it has some kind of worth.

People should stop and recognize
all of God's creatures no matter what size.

Mended Souls

When you feel that you are at the end of your rope
and no matter how hard you try you can not find hope.
Trying to find someone who you can talk to
who is kind and understanding when you are blue.

To help you deal with thoughts that run through your head
as you try to deal with things you dread.
With all your hurt and all your pain
as you try to keep them in refrain.

They help you talk of your painful years
so you can get past all of your fears.
With their help you can finally be free
by talking about your wishes and needs.

With letting them know what is deep in your soul
helps you realize that you truly are hole.
So when you really need a friend
they are the ones that your mind, heart and soul can mend.

Thanks to "The Mental Health Program"

Back Together

When troubles become to heavy to bare,
and you try so hard to find people who care.
When the feelings you have for the people you love
is not enough even with a slight shove.

That only makes the problems grow stranger,
and makes the ill feelings last even longer.
Just try to be patent day-by-day
as you pray each day the anger will not stay.

With feelings of anguish you try to avoid,
but with all of that you can not help being annoyed.
Trying to make things better for all,
but with each try all your hopes start to fall.

As you start building again with what little feelings you have
you begin to get really angry and mad.
Trying to deal and cope as you can
hoping you come up with a special plan.

To bring everyone back together
praying they stay that way forever.

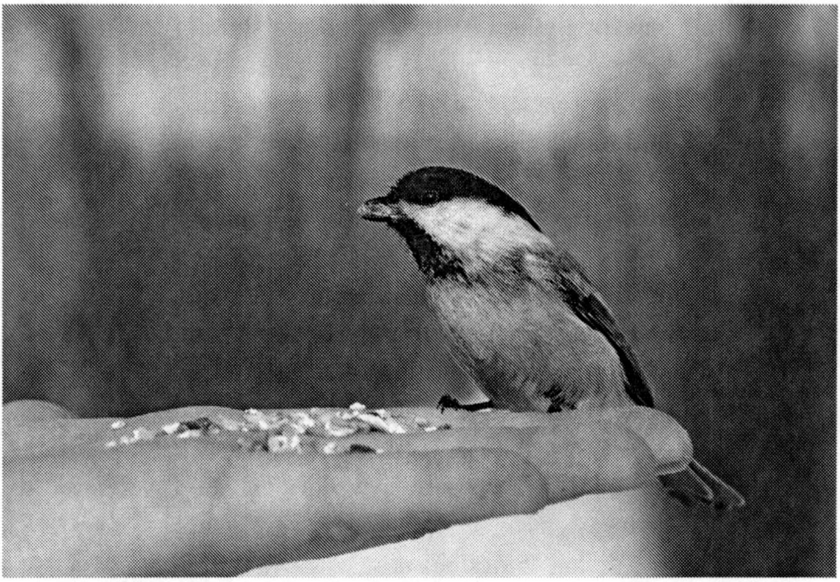

Your Tension

In the early morning hours
when the grass is covered with dew,
as the birds start to sing
like their songs are just for you.

As all wild life starts to come out
showing their beauty of life with out doubt.
From the sounds that they make to the way that they look,
each is unique as a newly written book.

Like the bird that gracefully glides across skies
as you watch in amazement as they pass by.
Then there are frogs and crickets by the score
that croak and chirp till the day is no more.

Then there are squirrels that run, frolic and play
up in the tree tops all of the day.
There are lots of others to numerous to mention,
and watching them takes away all of your tension.

Dangerous Opposition

As the fight inside yourself begins
you feel as if you will never win.
As you are torn apart by things then and now
you wish to forget, but do not know how.

Trying to search in extreme
to find out why you have those dreams.
The ones that terrify you so
with entrapment and fear that will not go.

As your running from people and things from the past
in the future they seem to catch you at last.
With ideas and thoughts that run through your head
that makes you think of things you dread.

As you wake up from nightmares that devour your hopes
as you fight everyday as your trying to cope.
The reality you live in by day is passion
at night in your dreams comes your dangerous opposition.

The poem "The Great Indian Chief" was published in The International Library of Poetry, the name of the book is "Dreams and Fantasies", published in 2001.

The Great Indian Chief

The Great Indian Chief who had lived a long life
waits for death to come and suffice.
As he stands on the edge of a cliff way up high
he seems to be a part of the sky.

Looking at his weathered face
seeing his glory and all of his grace.
You can see the warrior deep inside
as you gaze into his dark brown eyes.

He stands straight and strong as an old oak tree
you can see that his spirit is truly free.
As his long gray hair flows with the breeze
you can see his honor without a degree.

His courage is great as a grizzly bear
you can see it in his final stare.
As he raises his hands up to heaven above
the Great Spirit came down for his soul he did love.

My Guiding Star

Through all the years I lived at home,
and all the years I have lived alone.
You were there to help me on my way
keeping me safe each and everyday.

With kind thoughts and loving words
that each and everyone I heard.
From dawn to dusk you were there
letting me know how much you care.

In all the things you have said and done
that is what makes our family so fun.
With all the love you have inside,
and all the feeling you have of pride.

I am the proudest one by far for you Dad are
My Guiding Star.

Impatiently Waiting

As you are impatiently waiting to find out your fate
praying you find someone with the same traits.
Someone who thinks and feels as you do
is lonely and does not want to be blue.

Someone to share all the good times and bad
who will never really make you sad.
Someone you can tell you fantasies and fears
who will hold you when your eyes fill with tears.

Someone who will comfort you when things go wrong
as you make each other a little more strong.
Do not hide your feelings from one another
for that can only cause you both trouble.

Do not doubt, condemn or criticize
for you will lose your love before you realize.
So love each other with total honesty
so together you can set your hearts and souls free.

Loneliness

When the loneliness seems to tare you apart
from all the pain within your heart.
While your love is still trapped deep inside
with feelings that slowly destroys your pride.

As the inadequacy you feel everyday
comes with the things that people say.
You cope with the pressures the best you can
until you find a better plan.

When the paranoia and fears become unbearable
you pray that your inner soul is repairable.
As you dream of the way things could be,
but for now these things you can not see.

Someday you will find your one and only
from that day on you will never be lonely.

Desperate Decision

As my heart pounds hard with in my chest
my mind starts to throb so I can not rest.
I think of harsh words said in anger
as if they were said by a total stranger.

With moods as different as night and day
with hopes that the bad side will not stay.
With prayers filled with love for a better tomorrow,
but still they are filled with anger and sorrow.

With painful dreams that bring out my fears
as I watch in despair I can not think clear.
So with a heavy heart I go to the phone,
and sent my child out of my home.

Not forever, but for a short while
with prayers of hope that someday I will smile.
For my good and theirs I move on my notion
as Love guides my heart in this Desperate Decision.

Feelings Of Suffering

As the walls in my house seem to move in,
and the air in the room where I am sitting gets thin.
That is when my heart begins to pound hard and fast
it is then I wish for these feelings to pass.

As my chest seems to tighten with each breath of air
then I find that all I can do is stare.
So I look into space and time unknown
to find myself all alone.

As I see all my broken hopes and dreams
I also find others lies and schemes.
Trying to run to escape my fears
only helps bring out anger and tears.

As I try to look past all the anguish and woe
so these feelings of suffering will finally go.

Your One True Escape

When you cry inside where no one can see,
and you pray for your soul to be set free.
With the bondage of love, hate and despair
from these come a life which is very unfair.

The more you try to make life improvable
the more life becomes very unbearable.
For it does not matter how hard you try
in the end you always seem to cry.

When agony weighs heavy on your mind
it seems the answers you can not find.
Just keep looking for hope with each breath you take
for someday you will find your one true escape.

Life Stays The Same

As I sit ever so quietly listening to the sounds of the night
while the stars and the moon are with in my sight.
Creators of the night fills the cool night breeze
with soothing songs that echos off the trees.

The trees they look like hovering giants
in the dark their branches look so defiant.
As the darkness takes over my life once more
I wait for the light to even the score.

As the sounds of the night become sounds of the day,
and the sun gives out its elegant rays.
Only till night starts to fall once again,
and the darkness turns the light to dim.

At this point I know that life stays the same
along with the darkness and light lingers pain.

As Long As Hate Flows

When you hear harsh words and get angry looks
you pray for their end like a badly written book.
It seems the hatred goes on with a passion
as you try to change it with total obsession.

As you become more distraught with each sentence you hear
you pray with all your might to over come your fears.
Afraid to say anything that might set it off
as others around you seem to scoff.

It is hard for them to believe what you say,
but they will learn the truth one day.
Then all the anguish and sadness you have known
will leave you like a mournful moan.

Then maybe you can be happy again,
but you can not begin to know when.
As sad as it is this is the way that life goes,
and it will stay this way as long as hate flows.

Small Ray Of Hope

With all the hurt feels I get in a day
hugs should be given in the same way.
With all the beautiful things on earth
then why do people feel they have no worth.

It does not matter how hard I try
I always end up sitting alone as I cry.
With my memories of happier times
while I am haunted by others crimes.

So I give up all hope of finding true love
if someone gets near I give a backward shove.
To stay clear of the pain that might befall me,
but still I have hope of someday being free.

For without this small ray of hope in my heart
my life will end before it can start.

Differences

Why don't people stop and stare
to realize what it means to care.
To pick up a stone just to look at it
to see the wonders of each little bit.

As you hold it in your opened hand,
and see the differences in all stones where you stand.
Each is different in shapes, colors and sizes
people will then see many surprises.

For stones are large to small and pretty to plain,
but never will you find two precisely the same.
This is the way it is with people today,
but they should except the differences come what may.

For if they did the wars might end,
and everyone could end up as friends.
To love one another no matter how they look for a start,
and to all other people just open your heart.

With Heavy Hearts

Have you ever stopped to look at things
you never noticed before.
Like rocks, trees and even leaves
before they are here no more.

With so many kinds, in such large numbers,
but who really care or wants to bother.
All though there are people who could not care less
there are also those who feel they are blessed.

We should be glad God gave us so much beauty
to take care of it is everyone's duty.
To stop destroying all that lives,
and show that we are willing to give.

For people holds all of life in their hands
so what lives and dies is up to man.
They are devouring life as we know it today
by letting their values and love go astray.

As some of us watch with Heavy Hearts
as others tear this world apart.

First Love

When you fall in love for the very first time
you feel your world is so sublime.
Whether you are sixteen or sixty it really does not matter
yet if something goes wrong you could not feel sadder.

Then as the years pass and your still all alone
your heart feels as heavy as a very large stone.
As memories flow of that one special man,
and how he use to touch your hand.

You loved the way he caressed your face,
and you can almost feel his warm embrace.
Even though you have not seen him for years
you can still hear him whispering in your ear.

With a soft and gently voice when he talked,
but yet he had a tough guys walk.
You remember watching him walk away
as in your heart you prayed he would stay.

Yet one day he left and never came back
from that day on your world turned black.
As you are drawn to men that reminds you of him,
but they do not measure up and your heart goes dim.

You also remember the way by smelled,
and with a broken heart the tears do swell.
Then you realize he can not be replaced
so his memories you keep like a warm embrace.

A Special Man

When I think of him my heart does sigh,
because I miss him so I want to cry.
I think of how I touched his face,
and how it started my heart to race.

I love the way we could talk together
in all honesty not just of the weather.
I think of the gentleness deep inside
of this very big man that I care for with pride.

With a strong hand and soft spoken ways
he is respected as much as the suns life giving rays.
He is as generous as one person can be
helping people with all that they need.

I love to just sit quietly
with his arms around me he makes me feel free.
All my problems seem to disappear
at least for awhile as he held me near.

When this special Man came into my life
he helped me learn to deal with my strife.
With all the feelings of caring he showed
I can feel as my love inside for him grows.

Day-By-Day

As my spirit rises above myself into the eternal space
as I feel I am no longer in the human race.
My soul is torn between love and hate
these two emotions seem to control my fate.

Along with confusion and emotional strain
I can barely keep from going insane.
As tears and sobbing become my best friends
as I look to the future I can see no end.

With all my agony and all my pain
I try to keep myself in refrain.
As I sleep at night with hopes of forgetting the day
I dream of things that make my mind stray.

All those emotions that tear me apart
are ripping and shredding each day at my heart.
As I try to fight with each breath I take
I find myself with no escape.

So I will try my best to live Day-By-Day
in hopes of a better future along the way.

Sacred Indian Burial Grounds

The Indians have Sacred Burial Grounds
where their dead can be found.
It is a Holy place where their dead do lie
where family's at one time did cry.

As Indian's pray for the dead's living spirit to rise
from their bodies up to the clear blue sky.
As their dead lie beneath the ground
their presence can still be felt all around.

As their souls are trying to break free of this earth
to make peace an know all of their worth.
It is hard to rest as they're dead would like
for the living is threatening their sacred resting sight.

Spirits of the dead can not rest
with buildings lying upon their chests.
So leave them alone in their peaceful place
leave them their Honor and their Grace.

So all will know that they were here
as part of the history of our past years.

"Watch Over Me" was written for
Brenda Laycock, my beloved sister-in-law.
Who past away at the age of 42 with cancer.
Brenda was always there for me if I needed
someone to talk too. She helped me through
very hard times in my life. She was the most
caring and giving person I ever know.
This poem was published in The International
Library of Poetry, the name of the book is
"Timeless Voices", published in 2006.

Watch Over Me

Watch Over Me when things go wrong,
and my spirit is not so very strong.
Give me the strength to cope with life
to fight and conquer all of my strife.

Watch Over Me when I am confused
for these are the times when people abuse.
Let me know my friends from foes
yet give me love enough to show.

Watch Over Me while I am still alive
help me learn in all I do to survive.
To make this world a nicer place
for all that lives and the human race.

Watch Over Me still in death
as I take in all of my last breath.
When I clearly see my soul is set free
I can help someone else who will say
Watch Over Me.

Brenda Laycock

Mother Earth And The Indian's

As Mother Earth is home for all
the Indian people still recall.
They try to keep this land alive
so their future family's will not have to strive.

The Indian's land is sacred to them
the tree's, the grass and all things with in.
For nature and Indian's are one and the same
if you destroy one the other feels pain.

They take care of each other with deepest regard
for the future of man who is in disregard.
Everyday the earth does give of herself,
but it is not enough man wants more wealth.

So man keeps tearing and ripping away
as the Indian people are trying to pray.
To have them leave their land and them alone
before Mother Earth is, but a stone.

Where nothing will ever grow again,
and there will be no moon, sun or wind.
So let the Indian people have their land
for I believe that this is GOD'S plan.

Past, Present and Future

I wish that man would stop and see
just how much earth means to me.
All of life that roams this land
God put here for his special plan.

All with a purpose of their own
so man would never by alone.
Yet man abused, destroyed and betrayed
he tore up the earth to make it his way.

With no second thought about future life
or how much it would give all things strife.
It seems their love and compassion are gone,
and that makes hatred grow so strong.

So people that love and respect all that lives
will have to stand up and of themselves give.
To save the earth and all God created
so future generations will not feel degraded.

For what their ancestors did in the past,
and bring back Love and Peace at last.

The poem named "In The Indian's Shoes"
Was published in the International Library Of
Poetry. I did not buy the book, but I did
Buy the cassette tape. Where a professional
reader read this poem.

In The Indian's Shoes

When you talk about abusing the human race
the Indian people have had their share of disgrace.
As they fight for all they have in life
they can not defeat all of their strife.

So they try to live the best they can
until things change due to the white man.
When white man puts themselves in the Indian's place
I bet that they would lose all their faith.

When they feel the prejudice of other white man
they to would try to take a stand.
To fight for all that they believe
to have a life that they can conceive.

Where the abuse will end and love take priority
while they learn a hard lesson on authority.
Still until the day white man walks in the Indian's shoes
I think all races are destine to lose.

To My Daughter

To my daughter to whom I love so dearly
I pray for the day we can see things clearly.
When the love we have is the thing we show,
and all the bad feelings we have will go.

No longer to darken our family's door
so a happy life we will have once more.
With hard work, and the time we need
for our love and happiness to go to seed.

Then we will know all the good things we have
then we can get rid of all of the bad.
Until that day we will live separately
for we must get past our pain to truly be free.

We will get past it I know in my heart
at that point in our lives we can make a new start.

Allen, Tami & Matthew

To My Son

As I sit alone and think of you
my mind starts to wander and I feel so blue.
I miss the sound of your voice
I feel so alone by our choice.

I know you had questions you needed answers too,
but always remember my love for you is true.
I will always be here for you my son,
because our love for each other is as one.

So think of me when you are lonely and blue,
and I will be there in spirit with you.

Nathanial Allen Linna

Always Know

Always know that I am hear
when you need a friend to be near.
You helped me through some very hard times
as we talked and you smiled it made me feel fine.

With all the problems we have to deal with
we will still stick together and that is no myth.
So when things go wrong as they sometimes do
please remember I will always love you.

If you are ever feeling sad and blue
I will be with you in spirit this is true.

To my beloved sister "Roxie" who I love with
all my heart and soul.

*Together then,
Together now,
Together forever.*

Let's Try Peace

Saddam Hussein have you totally gone mad
to let destruction and war make you glad.
Does injustice and hate rule your cold heart
enough to tear your land apart.

To hurt and humiliate is your goal,
and sooner or later it will take it's toll.
I can not believe there is that much hate
in your cold heart is that your best trait.

Is love a word you just heard now and then
is this why you are determined to win.
Let's Try Peace, it is the best way in the long run
for nobody wins if they are holding a gun.

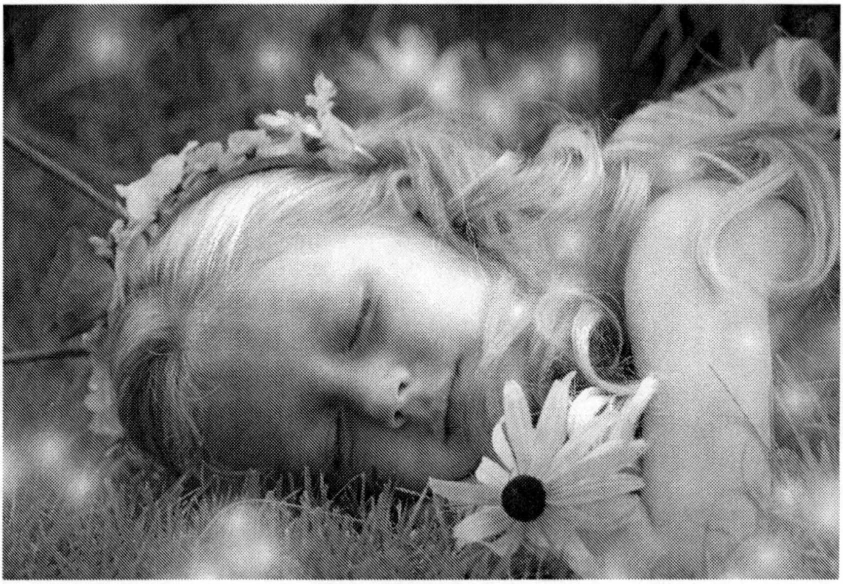

Peaceful Feelings

Have you ever sat in a field of green
all by yourself and do nothing but dream?
As you lie back in the long cool grass
to watch the weightless clouds go past.

Remembering happy times in your mind
waiting for better times you might find.
As the wind blows the grass you watch it sway
while listening to the song of a cheerful Blue Jay.

The sky is so blue you can almost see forever
as you watch in amazement with eyes that endeavor.
Then you close your eyes to hear the sounds
of the creators in the air and on the ground.

You will be surprised as to what you hear
the sounds of animals both far and near.
Lulling you till you are almost asleep
still you do not make a peep.

For the peaceful feelings you have found inside
you are afraid of losing when you open your eyes.

Invisible

While standing in a crowded room
invisibility fills my life with gloom.
Where words I speak are heard by none
as everyone there is having fun.

I am tired of being alone in a crowd
as I try to stand tall and be proud.
I feel as though I am not even there
all eyes see through me with empty stares.

How much can one person endure
I have taken to much that's for sure.
I think I have been ignored enough
I will say it with a voice that's gruff.

My statement will be loud and bold
so they will know that they were told.
So I can be seen for who I am
then I can live and be happy again.

All My Might

Even using all my might
it seems dissensions are winning this fight.
I fear the things running through my mind
although I can not stop them at this time.

With all the thoughts flowing in my head
makes me remember things I dread.
How to stop them I do not have a clue
I am afraid I do not know what to do.

I feel lost like a very small child
who is scared and has no one so the fear piles.
To the hindrance of losing my rationality
with all the corrupt acts impaled on me.

How do I erase these appalling memories
to try to set my mind and soul free.
I need a lot of help from above
to purge these persecutions and replace them with
LOVE!

Past Love

When you have loved somebody
who did not love you back,
the best thing for you to do
is get on a different track.

Do not plead, cry or beg of them
to try it one more time,
just go out and find someone else
who will be a lot more kind.

Someone who is sweet and sensitive
who will truly be your friend,
although it may be hard to find
someone that sweet and dear.

Do not give up all your hopes
for there is someone very near,
to help you through your harder times,
and fill you full of cheer.

For this has happened to me my friend,
and now my love is fear,
but now I have found someone so kind
to help me on my way.

He brings me joy and happiness
with every passing day,
I will tell you true, I was so blue
until he came my way.

Missing You

I miss you more then words can say,
and it is getting worse with each passing day.
Counting the minutes till I see you again
to give you the smile and hug I can not send.

While we are apart I can feel my heart
as it is breaking in two.
Loving you more then I can say
helps me make it through each new day.

So please remember and never forget
that my love for you I will never regret.

Emma & Eber Collins

The poem "Please Forgive Me"
was written after my Ma and Dad,
Eber and Emma Collins both past way!
It has helped me deal with things that were
done to me when I was little, Because I was
finally able to let go of those things.

Please Forgive Me

With my heart on my sleeve I think of you
I feel so confuse about what I should do.
You where my life line when you where alive,
but now you are both gone and I start to cry.

Even though we where miles apart
keeping in touch warmed my heart.
Now that you have gone to Heaven above
I needed to know that I am still loved.

Since you have passed from this world
I have told things that made my life unfurl.
I was afraid to tell you while you where alive
out of fear your love for me would die.

Please do not hate me for telling now
for if I had not, I could not feel proud.
The pride in me died years ago
when things went on that I could not show.

I was told that you would hate me so much
he used this phrase on me like a crutch.
So I let him do to me what he wanted,
and for years I have been ruthlessly haunted.

So please forgive me for what I have done
stay in my heart where we can be one.
Memories like these are terrible to have
help me forget them and please do not be mad.

I Will Be Gone

On the day that we meet
I found a love I could not forget.
When I walked along hand and hand
into the darkness with my man.

As we talked your feelings began to show,
but there are some things you will never know.
I have some secrets in my past
memories I pray will not last.

You see to a man I can not be true
I am afraid to love someone like you.
I could not stand to see you sad,
because of me that would be bad.

For this reason I am a loner
I can not let anyone become my owner.
I will stay with you for one night
to share my love before my flight.

So hold me now before the dawn
for when it comes I will be gone.

My Soul Cry's

There is someone I love, with all my heart
my soul cry's out now that we are apart.
We are apart from each other not by chance
we are separated now by circumstance.

When the enemy saw that he had his chance
Brenda he took you away in one quick glance.
He took you away not just from me,
but now I know you are now pain free.

For the pain that you endured in life
was more then all of my worse strife.
I know you are in a better place
for God is with you to keep you safe.

The fun we had then, are just memories
with pictures that show how it use to be.
You helped me through my hardest times
making me realize everything will be fine.

You tenderly touched my Heart and Soul
with your caring and love that will never
GROW OLD!

Humiliation And Hope

As humiliation and pain follow me
it almost brings me to my knees.
With all the hate that inside grows
it can only bring me sorrow and woe.

Someday I hope to get past this point,
but until that day I feel it in every joint.
With the thought of love I wish I had
so I would now have to feel so sad.

Someday all my dreams will come alive,
the thought of that helps me to survive.

Search For My Heritage

I know when and I know why
I feel as if I want to cry.
My Indian heritage I do not know
I wish to find out so I can grow.

The empty space inside of me
keeps my soul from being free.
To be able to have a fruitful life
so I can conquer all my strife's.

With questions I have still unanswered
I need to learn from my ancestors.
Lately I see things differently
then all my friends and family.

I feel things that are hard to explain
so I try to keep them in refrain.
There is life in everything on earth
I am learning to see all of their worth.

The tree's, the rock's, the grass and sky
thinking of these again I cry.
I see the destruction that is being done
to Mother Earth and Nature who are one.

So my need to learn of my heritage
just means that much more to me.
I want to understand all I can
so that I might try to make a plan.

To try to keep this land alive
so people on earth can learn to strive.
To help my family and friends survive
while keeping my soul and spirit alive.

Love Is A Feeling

Love is a feeling that everyone knows,
Love is a feeling that come's and goes.
This is the feelings I have for you
I hope very dearly you feel this way too.

I know that you do for you have told me so
now all I pray is that these feelings do not go.
We could be happy this is true
for you say you love me and I know I love you.

I have loved before and so have you,
but that does not mean that our love can not be true.
We will go out and have some fun
then maybe we will know if we can be one.

Maybe we can and maybe we can't,
but we will never know till we give it a chance.

The Hurt Inside

I cry alone in my lonely place
as sorrow fills my empty space.
As I am trying to deal with my pain,
and put my emotions in refrain.

Dealing with problems that come my way
makes me want to run away.
I am feeling like a child being punished
by things being said that's not so funny.

The hurt inside is growing stronger
as my spirit is feeling the pain even longer.
As I pray for the pain to go away
It seem to come back with each new day.

I give all the ones that are hurting me
to my savor so that my soul can be free.
So that I can be happy and laugh again,
and enjoy life till it comes to an end.

My Haunting Dreams

I feel that I can not speak my mind,
because thing said back to me are not kind.
It makes me feel like a little child,
and with that I can not smile.

The hurt and pain fills my head
which makes it hard to go to bed.
I go to sleep and dream of things
that in the day time nightmares bring.

To haunt my mind and soul till morning
with evil and hate that gives no warning.
So I tend to stay awake at night
to keep from facing my horrors and frights.

They try to make themselves at home
which makes my spirit, soul and mind roam.
As sleep takes over my body again
I fight to keep my dreams in refrain.

Sometimes I can and sometimes I can not
make my mind find a safe spot.
For memories of my happy times
so that once again I can feel sublime.

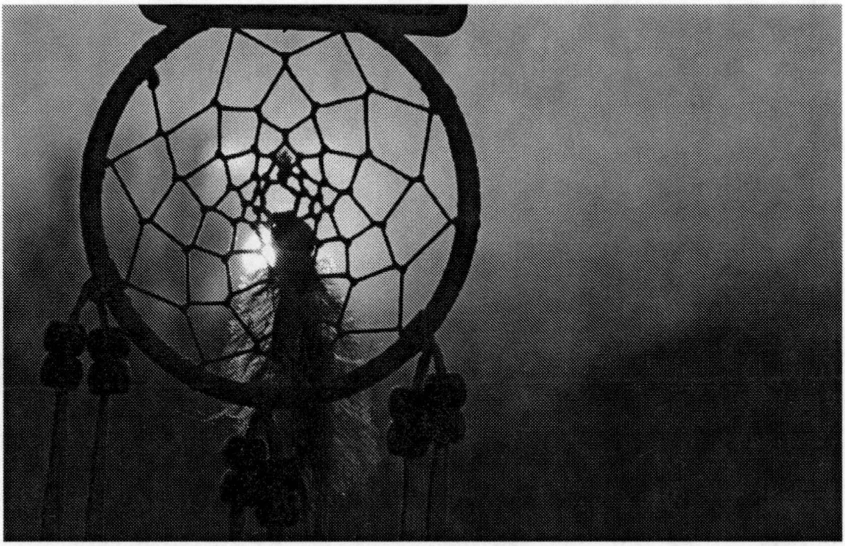

About The Author

Robin M. Morris raised three children by herself Allen who is now 32, Tami age 31 and Matthew now age 21. She loves them very much!

Most of the poems in this book were written at a time in her life when she felt hopeless. Robin wrote her poems between midnight and four or five in the morning. Do to frequent bouts with insomnia. Writing down her thoughts helped Robin get through some hard times. By putting her thoughts on paper Robin was able to release some of the stress within her with each word she wrote. Robin wrote her poems with positive endings, because that took away a lot of the hopelessness. It also gave her a glimmer of hope for the future.

Now after years of loneliness, pain, and insecurity Robin has the life she wanted so desperately and prayed so hard for. She is married to a wonderful man named Steve, whom she loves with all her heart. She has six grandchildren, three that are her son Allen's which she finally got to meet in the summer of 2006. Their names are Marisa, Elizabeth and Danielle, also Allen Jr. Robin's fourth grandchild from Allen who Robin meet in the summer of 1999. Steve and Robin adopted two of her grandchildren. Their names are Linna and Nathanial, they came to live with Robin and Steve when they were very young. Linna was almost 2, and Nathanial was about 10 months old. Linna is now 11, and Nathanial is 9.

Robin lives in Roscommon, Michigan with her husband Steve and their children Linna and Nathanial. She is very happy. Robin believes that if one of her poems touches someone's heart then all she went through when she was younger had a purpose. That purpose was to help people that feel they are at the end of their rope with no place to go. Robin wants to let those people know that if they will write their feelings down on paper, that will help them feel better, even get a positive perspective on their lives. The main thing Robin has learned is to give God all the thanks and Praise for all she has now, and all she will have in the future. By giving her a writing talent God answered Robin's prayers. This book of poetry is just one more great thing in her life. In Jesus name Amen!